Silent Ramblings

Love, Loss, and Triumph. A book of poems

Abed Mefleh

BookLeaf Publishing
India | USA | UK

Made with ❤ on the BookLeaf Publishing Platform
www.bookleafpub.in
www.bookleafpub.com

Dedication

I have a knack for getting into trouble for speaking the truth, which is exactly what led me here. The truth is, if it wasn't for the emotionally horrible experience of dating a narcissist and the ridicule that followed, I would never have shared my writings publicly. It was in doing so that I was able to get through the aftermath.

Wherever you are now,

get help, stop hurting others.

Preface

Sharing personal experiences with
narcissistic relationships can be quite
challenging, and the disbelief from others
can be disheartening. I have always written
poetry privately, hesitant to share due to
fear of criticism. However, my experience
with a narcissistic relationship and the
subsequent disbelief from others inspired
me to find my voice through poetry. Sharing
a poem online for the first time provided a
sense of being heard and a feeling of relief.
This collection of poems represents a
journey of healing and reclaiming my voice
amidst the challenges of a toxic relationship.
I am deeply grateful to my publishers for
their belief in my work and for providing me
with this opportunity to share my words.

In moments of deep heartache, there is a beauty found in the cracks. It's a reflection of the delicate balance between fragility and resilience. This shattered heart tells the story of pain transformed into strength, of a heart once broken but still enduring.

Each fracture represents a piece of the journey-a remembrance of lost love, a tribute to the trials faced, and the quiet power that emerges from sorrow. It carries the weight of your emotions, a delicate yet durable. A symbol of the beauty found in brokenness.

For those who find solace in darkness, let this remind you: Even in the shadows, light can still shine through.

Abed Mefleh

The Deceptive Smile

In the crowd, you wear your mask so well,
A smile that casts a beguiling spell.
They see the charm, the grace, the light,
But I see shadows in the night.

Your laughter rings, a siren's call,
Yet behind it lies a heart so small.
Narcissistic, you weave your tale,
Leaving others broken, frail.

You walk with an air of pure delight,
But your touch turns day to night.
Destruction follows where you tread,
A path of sorrow, tears unshed.

To the world, you're a shining star,
But I know the truth of who you are.
A facade of kindness, a cloak of lies,
Evil and darkness behind blue eyes.

Thank you

Thank you for letting me go,
For I would have never walked away,
I loved you too much to just let go,
Through the deceit, the tears, the fray.

Even when it hurt,
Even when I cried,
Even when we argued,
Even when you lied.

I promised you forever,
I was willing to stay.
But I owe you my gratitude,
For letting me go that day.

Let them think they have better,
Let them lose you,
Into the crowd,
Let them fade.

Let them believe,
Whatever they want,
Let them stray,
Carpe diem!
Come what may.

Aces and Eights

Round and round, the Devil and I,
In this game of shadows, we vie.
For far too long, we've dealt these cards,
I'm weary now, with a heart that's scarred.

In the Devil's game, I find my place,
A hand of fate, a losing race.
With aces high and eights in tow,
A dead man's hand, my fears bestow.

I played with Faith, my heart sealed tight,
Shadows crept in, the Devil smiles teeth
bright.
An ace of Hearts, he played so sly,
A raven-haired girl, and with her a lie.

She snuck into my guarded heart,
Her betrayal tore my world apart.
Now demons close, their whispers near,
In moments fraught with doubt and fear.

They circle 'round, they wait to see,
The moment when I fold, my soul no longer
free.
She never cared, it was all a game,
Well played Devil, Ace of Heart's cruel flame.

Her cruelty lingers, day by day,
Treating me as if I betrayed.
She cheated, lied, and did me wrong,
Yet blames me still, her voice so strong.

No light ahead, no path to see,
I call out to Him, please rescue me.
In this abyss, my voice I raise,
Deliver me from evil, this endless maze.

For though the Devil's hand is strong,
I need Your help, I can't carry on.
Through love's cruel game he made his play,
In my heart the Devil's finally found his way.

I feel the hatred, deep inside,
I need Your strength, help it subside.
I don't want to feel this way,
In Your Name O' Lord I pray.

The Quest

Paradoxical, the victim,
To cycle in, out, then back again.
For me, true connection is a rare,
Precious gem.

Never again will I settle,
Not for something less,
In matters of the heart,
I will not acquiesce.

I'd rather wait in isolation,
A lifetime long.
Avoid repeating the same mistakes,
Rushing into something wrong.

To feel truly captivated,
That's my quest,
Not just to feel needed,
but to find the best.

Each fleeting moment,
Not worth the hold.
Wasted on something so ordinary,
Someone so unspeakably cold.

I yearn for the extraordinary,
That heartfelt desire
A love that illuminates,
Two souls set afire

So here I stand, patient,
Eyes afire.
Refusing the mundane,
Yearning higher.

That true connection,
When it finally comes through.

Truth vs Lies

A battlefield in my head
Truth like a whisper unspoken
Lies like a flood unchecked
Every truth slowly broken

Dark shadows creeping in
Truth hides behind the curtain
Lies with their sparkling sin
Victory feels so certain

Torn between the light and dark
Truth struggles but seems weak
Lies paint a twisted arc
Every breath feels so bleak

I scream but silence follows
Truth buried under debris
Lies in its fine garb wallows
Destroying all that I see

Tangled in webs of deceit
Every step feels so hollow
Truth gets lost in defeat
Lies too bold to swallow

Searching for a glimpse of hope
Truth hiding in the shadows
Lies pull tighter the rope
Drowning in sorrows.

Brief

When I met them,
I didn't expect much,
They valued kindness,
A gentle touch.
Showed vulnerability,
Meant so much,
It set them free.
Unwavering empathy,
Quiet and strong,
Their heart soft,
They silenced the throng.
Even if it wasn't for long,
Faith and laughter,
Should have let it be,
Worst mistake of my life,
I'd rather death had taken me.

Karma's Whisper

In the hush between breaths,
Karma spoke,
A soft whisper,
yet crackling like smoke.

"You don't have to tell me,
Your tale of despair,
For I've witnessed their laughter,
That cruel, empty air."

"When your world turned to ashes,
They danced with delight,
But the tide swiftly shifts
Oh, how justice ignites."

"Now it's their turn,
To pay for their ways,
And it's their happiness,
I'll set ablaze."

"With an aura of vengeance,
I stroll through the night,
My shadow I cast,
On evil basked in light."

"I'm the balance you sought,
The wound that won't heal,
An echo of all that was stitched,
A look into the surreal."

"So, heed my words,
Like thunder they roar,
What's sown in the dark,
Shall be reaped at your door."

"For I am the storm,
Fools and their pride,
The flicker of wrath,
They can't hope to hide."

"I am Karma, relentless,
A queen without fear,
For in my embrace,
Echoes of vengeance draw near."

Harbinger of Misery

In shadows deep,
Deceit takes form,
A heart once pure,
Now weathered, worn.

Cheated and lied,
Behind your guise,
A web of secrets,
Spun with lies.

Backstabbed tender,
Trust betrayed,
In selfish acts,
True love decayed.

What was the point,
Of this charade?
One's moment of thrill,
One's future frayed?

The new man's heart,
It beats unaware,
Does he perceive it,
That lurking snare?
Does he know the truth,
Of how you tell lies,
No, that's how you get us,
The victim in disguise.

Yet know, dear friend,
I shall return,
A reckoning awaits,
For vengeance, I yearn.

For every wound,
each silent tear,
I will repay it fully,
Play upon your fear.

For in my grip,
The truth shall swell,
A harbinger of misery,
Bringer of hell.

Your chance at joy,
I vow to stain,
Your path to happiness,
Filled with disdain.

Parents Lament

In the quiet of dawn, shadows creep,
Life stirs, but my heart struggles to leap.
I wear a mask, painted with the guise,
While inside, a storm of sorrow resides.

Each breath feels heavy, a weight unkind,
Like air turned liquid, a cruel bind.
What was once gentle—a whisper of hope—
Now echoes the void, the unbearable slope.

Memories swirl like leaves in a gale,
Moments once cherished now frail and pale.
A love so profound, now scattered like ash,
A treasure, a heartbeat, forever to clash.

The world spins on, a chaotic flight,
While I stand still, lost in the night.
In crowded rooms, amidst joyful chatter,
Loneliness wraps me, silence grows fatter.

Hands that reach out, voices that melt,
But still, the isolation—deeply it's felt.

Words linger, lost, like dust on a shelf,
The unspeakable truth hides deep in myself.

In the kitchen, I pause, tears falling like rain,
Burnt offerings of normalcy, marred by the
pain.
Fingers crumble as breadcrumbs of days,
The flavor of grief seeps through all that I
taste.

I scream into silence, a wretched release,
Falling to fragments, longing for peace.
It's silent now, where footsteps once tread,
A symphony played by the ghosts in my head.

Demons waltz in with delicate grace,
Testing my spirit, a cruel embrace.
Each sigh questions the strength to remain,
Each heartbeat, a reminder of enduring the
strain.

Yet in this abyss where shadows entwine,
A flicker of resilience, a glimmer so divine.
Death whispers softly, promises of rest,
But life still stirs, a relentless quest.

So I learn to tread this shattered new ground,
Weaving love with loss, so hope can be found.
In the wreckage, a flicker of light,
A dance with the sorrow, the battle I fight.

The scars remain, etched deep in my core,
I'll carry a piece of you, forevermore.
In the tapestry woven of joy and regret—
This truth of my heart, I shall never forget

I hate that I still miss you

I hate that I still miss you, every single night,
I close my eyes, I can't escape the fight.
My body aches, my heart is torn,
For someone who's left me so forlorn.

You don't talk, you don't think of me at all,
Yet here I am, losing sleep, feeling small.
Discarded, forgotten, like I meant nothing,
While I'm left with these thoughts, constantly
bluffing.

Month passes to month, but pain remains,
I'm drowning in memories, wrapped in
chains.
You made me feel loved, then threw me aside,
Now I'm lost, with no place to hide.

The sun is gone., I just got out of bed,
Wishing these thoughts would leave my head.
I hate that I'm still here, feeling this way,
Longing for the one who led me astray..

Wizard of Narcissism

Dating a narcissist,
A tale so surreal,
Just like the Wizard of Oz,
The wizard isn't real.

The person we cherished,
They never existed,
A mirage of love,
That our hearts enlisted.

So real I wrote a poem,
On a card I had penned,
Sent with flowers to my love,
My own imaginary friend.

"Skin soft as moon lit rays,
Hair the color of night,
Eyes two stones, topaz,
Shining in the moonlight."

What if I told you the truth,
One to be revealed,
About the love we lost,
And the wounds we feel,

T'was born of shadows,
Nott of flesh,
A ghostly figure,
love's cruel jest.

They didn't leave us,
Didn't betray,
No lies, nor cheats,
That led us astray.

For how could one?
Cause such pain?
When they were never real,
Just love we imagined.?

A role they played,
With charm so slick,
A narcissist's spell,
A subtle trick.

It was always them,
Hiding from the start,
Preying on your needs,
With a falsified heart.

Realize the truth,
See the masquerade.
The Narcissist illusion,
End the charade.

Wake up, don't you see?
It's time to heal,
The wizard has spoken,
But the wizard isn't real.

The Mask Beneath the Smiles

Within the chambers of my heart,
A visage veiled, a work of art.
Trust shattered like the glassy dawn,
In quiet pain, my soul withdrawn.

To know the truth, yet feign my gaze,
In shadows deep, through endless maze.
No vengeful wrath, just whispers chill,
A bloodless war, my spirit still.

From depths of sorrow, no escape,
A mind entrapped in endless drape.
With haunted eyes, and heavy breath,
I walk the line between life and death.

In twilight's embrace, my solace found,
In silent night, my heart is bound.
Forlorn, I wander, lost, confined,
In death, the only peace I find.

Eclipsed by Temptation

I slept with the devil, her raven hair,
In blue eyes, enchantment—alluring snare.
The evil, deceptive, it danced like a wraith,
In beauty's embrace, concealed its own fate.

Charm wielded softly, charisma so sweet,
A whisper, a promise—compelling retreat.
Yet within that facade, dark shadows
entwined,
The devil's allure, my soul now confined.

Betrayal's kiss, a venomous sting,
In her web of deceit, I felt the sting.
Her lies, like poison, seeped through my
veins,
In her twisted game, I bore the chains.

She painted me black, the demon at fault,
While she danced in the light, free from
assault.
In the shadows, I linger, my heart torn apart,
Eclipsed by temptation, a fractured heart.

Another Life

A mirror cracked, where silence breeds
deceit,
Their laughter masks the shadows, cold and
fleet,
Between the lines of whispered lies, I stand,
Each flirt, each kiss, a trap set by their hand.

The child, a pawn in games of power's play,
With artful guile, they thread through night
to day,
But watch as secret lives unwind and bleed,
For emptiness demands they plant the seed.

Innocence lost, a heart torn asunder,
In the storm of lies, I stand and wonder.
A father's love, a distant, fading light,
In the grip of shadows, I lose the fight.

The child's eyes, once bright, now dim with
pain,
A silent cry, a tear in the rain.

In the web of deceit, we both are caught,
Another life, in darkness, fraught.

Veiled Lives

In shadows deep, the narcissist weaves,
A web of secrets none perceives.
Charmed nightly by their own despair,
They seek new victims everywhere.

So hollow, needing constant fills
They chase illusions, fill their thrills,
Flirting hearts, and funds like streams,
They build on ever-shifting schemes.

Behind the mask, another face,
The charm, the lies—an endless race.
New lovers lured to play the part,
Unknowing yet of webs and art.

When light reveals their empty core,
They flee to find an open door.
Your child becomes a weapon fierce,
To maim the love they cannot pierce.

In every heart, they plant their seed,
'Til love turns grief, and hope to need.
Oh, mortal soul, beware the guise,
Of twisted hearts and veiled lies.

Manipulative Mirage

Many nights, restless, beneath the dawn's
cruel light,
Dreams shattered by your deceptive plight.
Never did I foresee the depth of your guise,
Indifference cloaked behind those faithful
eyes.

Pained my heart with each blank gaze,
Unfazed by the torment that left no grace.
Lies danced from your tongue, a serpent's
hiss,
Alive only with your insidious bliss.

To you, my awoken agony meant naught;
In your game, love was never truly bought.
Vainly I yearned for some glimmer, some sign,
Emerging instead, betrayal so intertwined.

Belief in us was but folly, a sorcerer's cheat.
At every turn, my heart would vainly beat.
Caught in the web you spun with art,
Knives of deceit pressed against my heart.

Sympathy for the devil, you dared to claim,
Telling me love was but part of your game.
Apathy resided where care once slept,
Beneath your guise, your true nature crept.

Blissfully ignoring my calls, my pleas,
Indifference like a freezing winter's breeze.
No longer did my smile light up your night,
Ghostly your love became, then vanished
from sight.

Deceptive dreams you spun with ease,
Every excuse justifying your needs.
Vainly you cared for all that was mine,
In your own rules, you crossed every line.

Lying became the poison in our cup,
Feeding mistrust as I learned to toughen up.
Emptiness grew where once love thrived,
Emotions dwindled, no passion survived.

Life's fleeting whispers of love turned cold,
Inviting strangers into the space we
controlled.

Nonchalantly, you discarded me like dirt,
Gone was the warmth, replaced by hurt.

Feelings vanished as if they never truly were,
Oh, the pretense of love was now a blur.
Replay of a symphony, twisted and dark,
Gritting my teeth against your cruel remark.

Only time revealed your shallow deceit,
Two months, all it took for you to cheat.
Heartbeat hushed, my trust torn apart,
Exposing the fragile remnants of my heart.

At the beach, alone, I found no peace,
Cruel your absence, love's final piece.
Hollow vows in silence, we dissolved,
Empty echoes of love, never solved.

The Quiet Betrayals

In silence, you would always fade from sight,
No answering calls, no word, in darkest night.
With children planned, you'd flee without a
care,
While I stood waiting, longing you'd be there.

You danced with others, while my heart grew
cold,
Each absence marked, to another love you
sold.
When freedom came, like tides upon the
shore,
I matched your ways, in love's relentless war.

You screamed in fury, when truths were laid
bare,
Yet you desired my solitude, not share.
In turn, I found your friend in passion's blaze,
In mirrored actions, tangled in our maze.

We both have sinned within this tangled
trade,
Two hearts wrought heavy by the price we
paid.
Forever bound by silence and deceit,
In love's cruel shadow, neither found
complete.

The Hollow Soul

In shadows lurks the hollow soul,
Who bares their teeth in cruel disguise,
With venomed lies, their heart is coal,
Their conscience wrapped in thin, dark ties.

A blade concealed within their words,
They twists the truth without a care,
Throughout the land, deceit is heard,
From lips intent on foul affair.

A mind devoid of light or love,
They weave their schemes with tarnished
thread,
Scorns the trust bestowed above,
And leaves behind a trail of dread.

Beneath their grin, a void so vast,
Where morals sink in endless night,
With every tale and spell they casts,
They snuff out every hopeful light.

Beware the one who scorches trust,
And plants distrust within the heart,
For in their grasp, the purest rust,
And every bond, they'll tear apart.

A conscience lost is a deadly game,
A danger dressed in human skin,
For those who cheat without a name,
Bring suffering to kith and kin.

Elegy For my Father

I want to smile again,
Without the guilt or aches,
Miss you without crumbling,
For both our sakes.

Celebrate your life,
Without my heart breaking,
Grief's good side still elusive,
My spirit shaking.

Time hasn't eased the pain,
Some days it grows,
The path ahead stretches longer,
Still my Sorrow flows.

I resist joy,
Still in my own setting
Not ready to heal,
Too scared I'd be forgetting.

Let me sit here,
A moment's grace,
Things left unsaid,
Unspoken embrace.

Proud of you always...

Shadow in the Depths of Human Vice

In shadowy depths where whispers creep,
A figure marred by cruel deceit,
Once trust was there, now poisoned ground,
Her lies, a sordid, bitter feat.

In every gaze, a twisted truth,
A mirror chained to her own sin,
Each word she flung, a callous dart,
To pierce the fragile faith within.

Through nightly realms of false accuse,
I'll wear this stain upon my soul,
Her charm, a mask to hide all wrong,
Her darkness consumes what was whole.

Shared lovers close, a kin betrayed,
Each infamy a new lament,
In sickened hues their sin displayed,
My trust, so broken and so bent.

Each lie she told, a shard of glass,
This tapestry of shame and spite,
A soul devoid of empathy,
Her trail of pain, a wicked blight.

Insatiable her need to harm,
For validation crushed my core,
My boundaries were trampled there,
A heart bereft can feel no more.

And so in silent nights, I weep,
A shadow in her moral grave,
For trust once given, now is lost,
In depths of vices dark, depraved.

True Faithfulness

It's not just the bed you stay out of,
But the texts you never send,
The flirty chats you don't entertain,
The choices you defend.

It's the moments when no one's watching,
The lines you never cross,
The validation you don't seek,
That prevent a sense of loss.

It's the phone that's always open,
No secrets to conceal,
It's the trust you build together,
The honesty that's real.

True faithfulness is deeper,
Than just physical monogamy.
Without emotional integrity,
There never be true harmony.

The Veil of Truth

In darkened hearts, where secrets lie,
A whisper asks the reason why.
To seek the truth, or let it be,
Is knowing worth the agony?

The veil of lies, a manipulation of the mind,
A comfort false, yet so unkind.
For in the dark, we stumble blind,
Yet fear the light we seek to find.

The truth, a blade both sharp and bright,
It cuts through lies, reveals the night.
But once it's known, can we return,
To the blissful ignorance that we yearn?

To know the truth, a heavy cost,
For innocence, forever lost.
Yet in its light, we find our way,
Through shadowy nights to the brightest day.

So ponder well, for the choice is yours,
To seek the truth, or hide it behind closed
doors.
What's done in the dark will come to the
light.

For in the end, it's you who'll see.

It's the truth, and only the truth,
That will set your spirit free.

Ode to My Hatred's Flame

I hate

What you did to my soul,

I hate

That you don't even care,

I hate

How you only think of you,

I hate

The void of your mindless stare.

I hate

That you showed me my flaws,

I hate

How you roused this pain anew,

I hate

The smirk you wear with pride,

I hate

The Deceit that is you.

I hate

Your sweet lies to their ears,

I hate

The false tales that you spin,

I hate

The facades you craft so well,

I hate

The pity matches you win.

I hate

The sheer sight of your face,

I hate

your perfume's sickly smell,

I hate

How you use it to fuck all you chase,

I hate

Your voice; it's straight from hell.

I hate

More when you speak of love,

I hate

Your airs of grandeur high,

I hate

The betrayal you flaunt,

I hate

How you brazenly, blatantly lie.

I hate

The sexual sins you breed,

I hate

You blame all guilt on me to claim,

I hate

How you say I'm am the dangerous seed

I hate

You pretending to be hero in my daughters

name.

I hate,

How you fill me with grief,

I hate,

Your presence, no matter how brief

I hate,

The loathsome lies

Honestly, I hate you.

With or without your disguise.

The Broken

There goes my old cherished flame,
Another shining ring ascends in the frame.
Midnight vows now softly recede,
Promises melting in the starlight freed.

Once I burned with a gentle desire,
Now passion's ember sleeps in icy mire.
She marches boldly into the night,
Her footsteps resound fierce with might.

Behold us, restless dreamers in the deep,
Hearts chasing a peace too afraid to keep.
We welcome the art of the darkened part,
Loving wild wolves with an untamed heart.

Melodies echo our lamenting tune,
Feelings swelling beneath the silver moon.
Each morning, smiles cloak the inner fight,
We rise unwavering against the plight.

Grim days eclipse the promise of dawn,
Yet hope plants dreams on dew-kissed lawn.
Mythic tales lift our destiny's weight,
Where raw truth meets irony at fate's gate.

Never yield hope to the fury of the squall,
For the broken still rise,
Even when it's love that caused us to fall.

Funny to see you smile so bright

Funny to see you smile so bright,
A mask conceals your skillful play.
You mimic love, you feign delight,
He knows not yet you're made of clay.

Your words, like honey, sweetly drip,
He trusts the lies you softly say.
Unknowingly, on his love you sip,
He'll find out soon; you'll drift away.

Your past remains a secret trope,
A poor girl spun in web of woe.
You tell him tales devoid of hope,
His heart, naïve, begins to sow.

He sees a victim in distress,
A damsel waiting for her light.
But true, you are a dark recess,
Consuming everything in sight.

Your deeds, unknown, a hidden scar,
A veiled shadow in the night.
One day you'll stray a step too far,
And he'll uncover your cruel plight.

The same behaviors will take form,
Avoidance, blame—the ghostly scene.
He'll watch your love become a storm,
As you destroy what might have been.

Tales of mistreatment you'll recite,
A crafted story, dripped in lies.
He'll understand it all too late,
Through your false love, his spirit dies.

Whispers of Truth

In the shadows of deceit, I call you crazy,
Insecure, jealous, sensitive, to keep you hazy.
But beneath my words, truth mixed with lies,
A tapestry of complexity, woven with my
alibis.

"I lied to you," my actions scream,

"I cheated, disrespected, shattered your
dream."

"I abandoned you in your darkest night,

Twisted every argument, turned wrong into
right."

I made you doubt the strength you hold,
I isolated you, left your spirit cold.
I stole from you, not just things, but peace,
My grip on your heart, may it never cease.

By labeling you, I dismiss your pain,

Shift the blame, make you question your
brain.
Jealousy, I'll say, to justify my betrayal,
Too sensitive, I'll claim, to avoid my own tale.

But the truth stands tall, unwavering, clear,
My actions, not your emotions, are what you
should fear.
My lies, my cheating, my disrespect,
My abandonment, manipulation, I use all to
deflect.

But fear not!!

You are not crazy, nor insecure,
Not jealous, nor too sensitive to endure.
You are a survivor, a warrior, strong and true,
Deserving of love, respect, and a life anew.

Behind the smile

Every whisper in the dark,
A twisted tale unfolds,
Masking truth beneath a veil,
the secrets she withholds.

In shadows deep her deeds are done,
In daylight's blind disguise,
Luring trust with hollow words,
in webs of spun-up lies.

You think you know the heart within,
But tangled knots remain.
Hidden behind a smiling face,
her games are played so well,

Opulent praise she heaps on self,
 in tales she loves to tell.
Projection's art her chosen tool,
 to cast her sins away.

Knifing trust with subtle grace,
as love becomes her prey.
In every glance, a mirror shows,
 the faults of all but she,

Nefarious plots she weaves with ease,
To warp reality..

Shattered hearts, a trail of men,
All her legacy will be.

If I die

If I die, don't come to my burial,
Don't hide behind a veil of false tears.
If I die, don't spend on a casket imperial,
When you could have cared through the years.

Don't waste on a hearse so grand,
When I walked alone in the rain.
If I die, don't wear black bands,
For it's the true color of your disdain.

Don't tell my lifeless form you'll miss me,
When you did so little while I breathed.
If I die, don't cover my grave with glee,
With flowers you never bequeathed.

Don't post your RIP messages in haste,
When you ignored me in life's strife.
If I die, don't pretend with such waste,
For you missed your chance in life.

Elegy for a Dead Dream

As days go by, the dream won't die,
Once filled with light, now shadows lie.
The tears you shed, a cunning guise,
Making me feel like the bad guy.

It's over now, I must move on,
Can't bear the weight, love's ghost is gone.
I gave my all, but now I see,
The time has come to set you free.

We can't go back to what we were,
The pain is flames, too fierce to cure.
Scars and ruins are all I see,
Wish I could erase our history.

Inside I knew, the end was near,
Can't bear this life, can't stand the fear.
I fucking hate you for your lies,
For treating me like some disguise.

I don't want words to mend this rift,

Inner peace, my only gift.
Can't fake love like you always do,
Goodbye forever, I'm through with you.

I'm Not Mad

I'm not mad, I'm just done,
Always battles fought, but never won.
Not angry, just weary, you see,
Of giving all, yet never free.

I'm done with the endless strife,
The constant drain on my life.
Done with those who take, not give,
Who drain the joy from the life I live.

I'm not mad, just stepping away,
From those who'll darken my day.
No more will I fight this fight,
For peace is my guiding light.

I'm done with the ones who don't care,
Who never see the love I share.
Done with the effort, the endless try,
It's time to bid these ties goodbye.

I'm not mad, just finished, it's true,
With those who never see me through.
Family, friend, or fleeting bond,
I'm done, and now I move beyond.

When I'm gone

When I'm gone, will I be missed?
Or am I just a shadow in the mist?
A nameless face in the crowd,
Lost in silence, never loud.

I don't know why I exist,
A soul adrift in a dark abyss?
I never asked to feel this pain,
A heart caught in a ceaseless rain.

I don't want to feel this way,
Trapped in night, devoid of day.
Will anyone remember my name,
Or will I vanish, just the same?

The Deceptive Smile

In the crowd, you wear your mask so well,
A smile that casts a beguiling spell.
They see the charm, the grace, the light,
But I see shadows in the night.

Your laughter rings, a siren's call,
Yet behind it lies a heart so small.
Narcissistic, you weave your tale,
Leaving others broken, frail.

You walk with an air of pure delight,
But your touch turns day to night.
Destruction follows where you tread,
A path of sorrow, tears unshed.

To the world, you're a shining star,
But I know the truth of who you are.
A facade of kindness, a cloak of lies,
Evil and darkness behind blue eyes.

Wisdom, Time and Pain

Maturity unfolds with patient grace,
A journey etched in lines upon our face.
Through trials faced and lessons learned anew,
We grow into the wisdom that is true.

We seek not loyalty from hearts astray,
But find our strength in walking our own way.
The lies we hear from those who cannot see,
Reflect the inner truths they fear to be.

Peace is born from battles fought within,
A quiet calm where understanding begins.
Maturity, the art of letting go,
Of seeking more than others can bestow.

In growing, we embrace our inner might,
And learn to stand alone in darkest night.
We see the flaws in others, and in self,
And find in both a source of boundless wealth.

For wisdom is the gift of time and pain,

A treasure earned through loss, through gain.
Maturity, a beacon shining bright,
Guides us forward with its gentle light.

Chasing Shadows

I just want to be loved, I plead,
Does anyone else feel so lone?
Like my presence is just a ghost,
In a world where I'm yet unknown?

Always chasing, hearts on my sleeve,
Hoping they will love me as true,
But no matter how hard I try,
Never enough, my spirit blue.

I know we all have our tributes,
Everyone has their fight to face,
But understanding dims my pain,
Still, it leaves such an empty space.

I try to give the best of me,
Striving always to be so kind,
Yet I feel worthless, through and through,
An endless void within my mind.

I could hug a cactus for years,
Endure each thorn just to belong,
Embracing pain to feel the love,
To find meaning where I feel wrong.

Am I too much, or not enough?
Lost in this question night and day,
Maybe love is not in my fate,
Only to fail, and fade away.

In twilight's grasp

In twilight's grasp, your phantom stays,
A ghost that chants through endless days.
Though footsteps wander, far and wide,
A part of me has also died.

Why you linger, the answer's veiled,
In love's grip tight, where once prevailed.
The first touch cold, the first song stilled,
In you, my faith forever chilled.

Though paths now veer to distant parts,
I can't extract you from my heart.
Unconditionally, my spirit bends,
To scars that time never mends.

The only love to cut this deep,
In waking hours, in dreams I weep.
Each tear I shed, each breath I make,
A testament to this heartache.

So here I stand, on life's long stage,

Murdered memories, now endless rage.
Gave me a smile, to watch it decay,
Then with greatest ease, you turned away.

The Illusion's dance

In twilight's glow, I found your eyes,
A lure so bright, it masked the lies.
Your whispered words, a serenade,
In shadows, our destinies played.

You spun a dream of tender care,
With every breath, I lingered there.
Hopes burgeoned like the morning sun,
But vanished once the day was done.

You voiced affection, crafted ties,
Yet all were woven from thin guise.
I fell, entranced by phantoms' call,
Not knowing I was meant to fall.

When dawn revealed night's cruel deceit,
You vanished swiftly with no retreat.
Heart shattered in the silent room,
Where once was love, now lingers gloom.

You let me dream of love divine,
But cast me off, your heart malign.
You taught me to trust, then scorched it
through,
Left me alone amidst the rue.

The pain is more than wounds of flesh,
It's every promise turned to ash.
Not for the love that wasn't true,
But for the act you let me view.

Now in the night, my thoughts retrace,
The dance of shadows, your embrace.
I'm not enraged by love's demise,
But by the mask, and your disguise.

The Ballad of Broken Vows

In twilight's mist, where shadows creep,
Emma Lee wove secrets deep.
She spun her tales, a silken thread,
Binding hearts with words unsaid.

Beneath the moon's pale, mournful light,
She whispered truths, then took to flight.
A silver tongue, sharp as a blade,
In darkness, fragile trust she swayed.

From lips of roses, lies did bloom,
In every kiss, deceit found room.
She played her part upon love's stage,
A gypsy heart, locked in a cage.

Her promises, mere phantom dreams,
Eclipsed by night's deceitful schemes.
With every touch, a scar she'd weave,
The sorrow that she couldn't leave.

Hidden truths, like stars concealed,
Within her eyes, unhealed, revealed.
A siren's song, a siren's snare,
Entwined in threads of dark despair.

The dawn would break, and vows be torn,
In silence, lovers left to mourn.
For Emma Lee, a fickle name,
Now lost in echoes of her shame.

So, let this tale, in whispers live,
Of hearts betrayed and none forgive.
Recall her face, a mask of sin,
Where love's true heart could not begin.

The Siren's Song

In whispers soft, like the faintest breeze,
Emma Lee spun her web with ease.
With eyes that sparkled, mask in place,
She danced through hearts with fleeting
grace.

Her woe-laced tales, so finely sewn,
Of lovers past, each cruel as stone.
She took my hand, her voice was sweet,
And painted lies of past deceit.

She claimed her heart was bruised and
scarred,
That love had left her deeply marred.
Her stories crafted, false and neat,
A labyrinth of bitter sleet.

I was the hero to her cry,
Her former lover, branded lie.
But once she had my trust in hold,
Her true intentions did unfold.

The truth she hid, like shadow's sweep,
Beneath her smile, a secret deep.
She played the victim, worn and frail,

Yet schemed beneath her fragile veil.

As soon as I was empty, used,
Her next deception was infused.
She turned to him, her eyes aglow,
And cast me out, her heart of snow.

She told him tales of twisted past,
That I was cruel and love couldn't last.
And once again, her mask in play,
She lured him close to her dark sway.

But he will see, as shadows break,
The real truth behind her ache.
And he will suffer, just as I,
Beneath the spell of Emma Lee's lie.

For tangled webs she weaves, behold,
Within them lies her heart, grown cold.
Those entrapped taste in pain and vice,
The bitter chill of Emma Lee's ice.

Emergence

One of the harshest lessons,
It's painfully clear.
Is learning to fall out of love,
With illusions held dear.

Expectations I harbored,
In those few, I held tight,
Their promises frigid,
Fleeting winds on a cold night.

Potential and promise,
Hypotheticals, untrue,
For so long I've settled,
Accepted much less than due.

But now I'm moving forward,
No longer in a loop,
Embracing my own worth,
Reclaiming my own truth.

I've stifled my spirit,
Bit my tongue till it bled,
Bowing to others' whims,
In defiance now I tread.

Saying "no" to those
Who never saw my sacrifice,
Now I say "yes" to myself,
And that feels so nice.

This is not a restart,
I'm not turning back.
I won't reduce myself,
Helping others feel less slack.

I've outgrown you,
And the control you claimed,
And now,
In my own worth,

I am free

My soul's unchained.

Untitled

In the quiet of dawn, shadows creep,
Life stirs, but my heart struggles to leap.
I wear a mask, painted with the guise,
While inside, a storm of sorrow resides.

Each breath feels heavy, a weight unkind,
Like air turned liquid, a cruel bind.
What was once gentle—a whisper of hope—
Now echoes the void, the unbearable slope.

Memories swirl like leaves in a gale,
Moments once cherished, now frail and pale.
A love so profound, now scattered like ash,
A treasure, a heartbeat, forever to clash.

The world spins on, a chaotic flight,
While I stand still, lost in the night.
In crowded rooms, amidst joyful chatter,
Loneliness wraps me, silence grows fatter.

Hands that reach out, voices that melt,
But still, the isolation—deeply it's felt.
Words linger, lost, like dust on a shelf,
The unspeakable truth hides deep in myself.

In the kitchen, I pause, tears falling like rain,
Burnt offerings of normalcy, marred by the pain.
Fingers crumble as breadcrumbs of days,
The flavor of grief seeps through all that I taste.

I scream into silence, a wretched release,
Falling to fragments, longing for peace.
The silence responds, an echo of dread,
A symphony played by the ghosts in my head.

Demons waltz in with delicate grace,
Testing my spirit, a cruel embrace.
Each heavy sigh questions the strength to remain,
Each heartbeat a reminder of enduring the strain.

Yet in this abyss where shadows entwine,
A flicker of resilience, a glimmer divine.
For while death holds soft whispers of rest,
Life still stirs, a relentless quest.

So I learn to tread this shattered new ground,
To weave love with loss, where hope can be
found.
In the wreckage, a flicker of light,
A dance with the sorrow, a battle, a fight.

Though the scars remain, etched deep in my core,
I carry a piece of you, forevermore.
In the tapestry woven of joy and regret—
This truth of my heart, I shall never forget.

Thank You

Thank you for letting me go,
For I would have never walked away,
I loved you too much to just let go,
Through the deceit, the tears, the fray.

Even when it hurt,
Even when I cried,
Even when we argued,
Even when you lied.

I promised you forever,
I was willing to stay.
But I owe you my gratitude,
For letting me go that day.

Let them think they have better,
Let them lose you,
Into the crowd,
Let them fade.

Let them believe,
Whatever they want,
Let them stray,
Carpe diem!

Come what may.

Love's Fight

Some dream of love that's always bright,
But shy away from stormy nights.

They crave the joy, the endless cheer,
Yet flee when hard times draw too near.

They seek relationships free from strife,
A perfect, easy, flawless life.

But love, true love, is not so neat,
It has moments, hardships, it's bittersweet.

For love is more than sunny days,
It's holding on through darkened haze.

It's standing firm when differences roar,
And finding the strength to love once more.

It's in the tears, the fights, the pain,
The times you think it's all in vain.

It's weathering the fiercest storm,
And finding peace when hearts are warm.

So if you seek a love that's true,
Embrace the trials you must go through.

For nothing good is ever a breeze,
And love's worth is never found with ease.

Hold tight to those who share your fight,
Who stand by you through the darkest night.

For in the end, it's worth it all,
To rise together, and never fall.

Karma's Whisper

In the hush between breaths,
Karma spoke,
A soft whisper,
yet crackling like smoke.

"You don't have to tell me,
Your tale of despair,
For I've witnessed their laughter,
That cruel, empty air."

"When your world turned to ashes,
They danced with delight,
But the tide swiftly shifts
Oh, how justice ignites."

"Now it's their turn,
To pay for their ways,
Watching as their happiness,
Is set ablaze."

"With an aura of vengeance,
I stroll through the night,
My shadow I cast,
On evil basked in light."

"I'm the balance you sought,
The wound that won't heal,
An echo of all that was stitched,
A look into the surreal."

"So heed my words,
Like thunder they roar,
What's sown in the dark,
Shall be reaped at your door."

"For I am the storm,
Fools and their pride,
The flicker of wrath,
They can't hope to hide."

"I am Karma, relentless,
A queen without fear,
For in my embrace,
Echoes of vengeance draw near."

The Harbinger of Misery

In shadows deep, deceit takes form,
A heart once pure, now weathered, worn.
Cheated and lied, behind your guise,
A web of secrets, silk spun with lies.

Backstabbed tender, trust betrayed,
In selfish acts, true love decayed.
What was the point of this charade?
One's moment of thrill, one's future frayed?

The new man's heart, it beats unaware,
Does he perceive it, that lurking snare?
Does he know the truth, of how you tell lies,
No, that's how you get us, the victim in disguise.

Yet know, dear friend, I shall return,
A reckoning awaits you, for vengeance I yearn.

For every wound, each silent tear,
I will repay it fully, play upon your fear.
For in my grip, the truth shall swell,
A harbinger of misery, Karma's ringing bell.

Your chance at joy, I vow to stain,

Your path to happiness, filled with disdain.
For behold a pale horse, the rider is death,
And in my wake, there will be nothing of you left.

Frienemies

In my final act of love,
I set you free
No more calls or texts,
Just strangers, you and me.

I won't hover over your name,
No need for this refrain.
I'll erase you from my contacts,
Just a stranger is all memory retains.

You deserve a life,
Without my constant plea.
For attention, for change,
For begging, you to see.

I truly am sorry,
For drowning you with my love.
When all you ever wanted,
Was to be placed above.

I watched you build walls,
While I built fragile bridges.
I watched you turn cold,
Scars of unresolved past ridges

Fearing one wrong word,
You'd run away.
I tiptoed around your silence,
Day by day.

Unbeknownst to you it hurt,
More deeply than words could convey.
Yet I persisted in silence,
Hoping you'd choose to stay.

Now clarity unfolds,
And here's my final vow:
I release you completely,
Will you please go now?

I won't reach out,
I won't remind you.
Of what you lost,
Of what we left behind.

You're free in the end,
From my love's fold.
For my final act,
No longer will I pretend.

That we...
Were always...
Just strangers....
More foe than friend.

Frozen Mirage

Whatever negative energy stirs within,
Keep it locked away, let no one in.
The chill in your gaze, striking and clear,
Is this your true essence drawing near?

Removed and remote, you silently reside,
Is this the self I cannot abide?
Let the shadows preserve your frozen guise,
While the secrets of your heart continue to hide.

You never loved me, yet you lingered still,
Riding my pulse until trust did kill.
Time after time, you shattered my song,
Yet I embraced the pain, I played along.

You battle with detachment, a truth so plain,
Drifting from love like debris in the rain.
You feigned concern, offering empty care,
Only to vanish into the cold night air.

You bestowed a hope, a mirage unseen,
Aware that its light would never convene.
I shun the deceit spun in your hold,
Giving false hope, could you be any more cold?

The Ballad of Deceit

In days of yore, where shadows call,
Emma Lee's love did rise and fall.
She wooed me with her angel's guise,
Beneath the veil, a serpent lies.

She spun her webs of sweet deceit,
Left former love in ruined defeat.
Her art of lies, a cruel ballet,
In darkness, truth would lose its way.

Her eyes did shine with feigned remorse,
A victim's tale, her sole recourse.
She whispered secrets, hid the truth,
With artful grace, she stole my youth.

Fair Emma Lee, with voice so sweet,
Did weave her tale, my heart's retreat.
Her former love, the villain cast,
And I, the savior of her past.

But lies have wings, they could not stay,
The truths she buried found their way.
She left me shattered, cold as stone,
Her mask now gone, I stood alone.

Now to another she has fled,
With tales of woe spun from her head.
He'll find her gentle eyes untrue,
And suffer as I've suffered too.

Truth vs Lies

A battlefield in my head,
Truth like a whisper unspoken.
Lies like a flood unchecked,
Every truth slowly broken.

Dark shadows creeping in'
Truth hides behind the curtain.
Lies with their sparkling sin'
Victory feels so certain.

Torn between the light and dark'
Truth struggles but seems weak.
Lies paint a twisted arc'
Every breath feels so bleak.

I scream but silence follows,
Truth buried under debris.
Lies in its fine garb wallows,
Destroying all that I see.

Tangled in webs of deceit'
Every step feels so hollow.
Truth gets lost in defeat'
Lies too bold to swallow.

Searching for a glimpse of hope'
Truth hiding in the shadows.
Lies pull tighter the rope'
Drowning in sorrows.

Scars

When will you stop blaming me,
For all the pain I've received?
When will you stop accusing me
For all that we've conceived?

When will you choose to understand
The depth of what I feel?
We both crave peace of mind,
Yet wounds we never heal.

We fight and hurt each other,
both too scarred to bend,
You knew my vulnerability,
Yet chose to break, not mend.

You said you knew my fragile heart,
Yet caused it endless ache.
How could you claim to love me,
Then watch my spirit break?

You used my open heart
To tear my soul apart,
How could you say you care,
Hiding secrets in the dark?

I wish you'd warned me,
Loving you would bring such endless pain.
In my heart, I've loved you deeply.
My mistake, you made it all in vain.

You made me feel so small,
Like nothing I did was right.
You blamed me for our downfall,
And dimmed my inner light.

I would've done it all for you,
But you took me for granted,
Now I'm tired of the hurt,
And the love that's so slanted.

Can you even stop,
Blaming others for your tears?
When will the cycle stop,
Hurting others because of your fears?

I long for peace and healing,
For love that's truly kind,
But with you,
I only found the scars you left behind.

Whispers in the Shadows

In shadows where secrets softly tread,
We are whispers, barely said.
Not lovers bound by constant need,
Nor friends with benefits, indeed.
No sweet nothings, no songs to share,
Just fleeting moments, raw and bare.
A touch of lust, a spark of fire,
We meet, we part, simply carnal desire.
Betraying another, in secret our place,
Behind one's back, another's face.
Not quite something, almost there.
We are nothing, only a glimpse of what we do not dare.
We are nothing, we are free
In the shadows, disregarding accountability
Desire, lust, passion, we choose to be.

The problem

This will cut deep, but truth be told,
Admit your wrongs, stop the charade,

Be bold.

You moved foul, left scars behind,
Yet you play the victim, acting blind.
You lost it all, those who truly cared,
But you pretend, as if it were you ensnared?

Surrounding yourself with cheerleaders of deceit,
Instead of facing the truth, admitting defeat.
It's time to own up, confront your lies,
Stop hiding behind a mask, drop the disguise.

Seek the truth, find genuine aid,
Before your integrity completely fades.
No more delusions, your evil game.
Face your actions, accept the blame.

Only then can you begin to heal,
And find a life that's honest and real.

Nature's Veil

Nature's beauty, a deadly guise,
A supernova's burst, a hurricane's eyes,
Tiny tree frogs, vibrant yet sly,
From afar, they captivate the sky.

Enchanted by beauty from a distance,
Drawn in by allure, unaware of resistance,
Until we get closer, the danger revealed,
What it is doesn't make it concealed.

You were my supernova, my hurricane's calm,
A vision of splendor, a siren's sweet song,
I fell for a version that never was true,
A mirage of you, where I didn't belong too.

Your intentions weren't evil, just nature's design,
A force to be reckoned, a line to define,
I loved what I saw, not what was inside,
Nature's beauty, a deadly guise.

Echos of us

How do you lose a person so utterly and true,
That even their essence fades from view?

How can it be that all we shared,
Vanishes, as if it was never there?

Memories once vivid, nowhere in sight,
Our laughter and tears, merely echoes in the
night.

Everything we were, now whispers in the wind,
A story untold, where do we begin?

To think we were once so intertwined,
Now nothing but strangers, with no ties that
bind.

How odd it is, this twist of fate,
To become strangers again, and at such a rate.

Yet in the silence, faint echos remain
The reminder in the form of pain.

Though we are lost, and paths diverge,
In my heart, the pain will always surge.

An epitaph of love

In shadows drawn by hearts confined,
A love misshaped, the soul maligned.
Her gaze, a shard that grips his pain,
Reflecting truths he can not restrain.

Through murmurs cruel, his fears take bloom,
Each doubt she stokes, a seed of gloom.
Her touch, a chain that binds his breath,
Their love, an omen veiled in death.

His longing screams, a silent plea,
Clings to the void, "Why can't they see?"
Yet still she drinks, his essence fades,
To dust, to dusk—his light decays.

She sows the thought, "You are too much,"
But cannot give, no healing touch.
A phantom he weeps, all hope he withdrew,
His broken heart cries, "Love is cruel."

Dreams bleed to black, his soul now too,
Beneath the weight, the sky's a cold hue.
Shadows stretch long, mornings are few,
In silent whispers, echoes now grew.

Fragments of hope, now scattered, askew,
Wandering through nights, lost and forlorn.
Seeking solace from the pain he'd borne,
In each tear, a story of love's mourn.

Yearning for dawn, he embraces the storm.
With each breath, the weight of despair grows.
A life now barren, where love's river once flowed,
In the silence, his final verse will compose.

An epitaph of love, where heartache arose.

"Goodbye, dear world," with last breath he sighed,
"My heart once full, now broken inside."
"In hell's keep, my soul will reside,"
"Remember me, the tears now dried."

A lament eternal, in darkness confined,
The echoes of love, a ghost left behind.
In shadows deep, my soul shall bind,
An end to my tale, forever entwined.

Ghost and Gaslights

In my rough spot, you turned away,
Felt neglected, chose not to stay.
You punished me in silent ways,
Through sunshine and darkest days.

I tried to leave, you'd give me hope,
A dangling line, a fraying rope.
Mental torture, truth concealed,
You didn't want what was revealed.

You played the innocent, so sly,
While blame on me you would imply.
I lost my trust, my faith in you,
And still you ask me, "Why, oh why?"

For when your mind to darkness fell,
I stayed and held you through the hell.
But when my world was torn apart,
You let neglect consume your heart.

Hard it seems for you to admit,
You didn't love, you couldn't commit.
I didn't matter, you see, it's clear,
Love vanished when I needed you near.

Faith without Integrity

If someone can rise close to you,
The fault lies not in love's past true,
But hearts that drift in careless tide,
Fickle wavers by their side.

An interloper casts their spell,
Their role ignites a gleaming hell,
Yet none can breach two hearts entwined,
Unless trust's thread is undermined.

The partner weak in ways they dwelt,
In open realms, their folly felt,
While those who tempt and breach the line,
Commit a sin by design.

Respect demands you step away,
Integrity must hold its stay,
From bonds where hurt takes root and grows,
A truth where only sorrow knows.

Competing souls for hearts impure,
Should learn the pain they can endure.
For faithful hearts, respect retains,
Boundaries set, love remains.

Walk from shadows, mend the breach,
Respect yourself, do not beseech.
Worth is not in tearing down,
Nor in love that wears a frown.

It's not for you to heal their shame,
Nor labor under love's sad name.
You cannot chain a heart in flight,
But cherish those who'll stay and fight.

For true respect comes from within,
Aligned with love, devoid of sin.
Thus in this ballad, hear the plea—
Integrity means fidelity.

The Parasite Behind the Mask

A love once wrapped in golden glow,
A thorn did mask the rose's plea.
The nectar once seemed pure and sweet,
Yet bled my heart, unseen to me.

You think you lost the love so true,
A phantom's touch, its sting is gone.
The parasite but feigned delight,
Whilst feasting on my breaking dawn.

No soulmate's hand did grasp my soul,
A predator in charm's disguise.
Their gentle kiss was poisoned breath,
Their eyes the veil to twisted lies.

With promises as empty as,
The echo where my dreams did lie.
The vows were but a hollow tune,
A script rehearsed with each goodbye.

They fed upon my light inside,
Their shadow dark, a void remained.
My spirit weary, plucked and torn,
My sense of self by frailty stained.

The mask has slipped, the truth unveiled,
Their essence, cold and stark remains.
The tender act, a fleeting mist,
Now shatters under grief's refrains.

Release the fantasy you held,
Let healing balm your wounded pride.
For what you lost was not your love,
But the parasite that thrived inside.

Their Goal

The goal was to break you, to watch you fall,
Go back to your old ways, you'd end it all.
But you rose from the ashes, defying their
schemes.
Turning their darkness into delusional dreams.

As a Trojan horse, you did arise.
Planted in their midst, a cunning disguise.
God's design, a masterful plan,
Allowed it to unfold, in the face of man.

Back into the flame, back into the den,
Emerging stronger, leading wolves then.
They thought you'd be devoured, by their misery,
broken, bent.

But now they see the strength you were meant.
God's been with you, through every trial,
You faced it all, without guile.

Always helping, even those who opposed,
With love and kindness, you composed.
Chosen amongst them, for your pure heart,
No arrogance, no ill intent did you impart.

Loving people, even false friends,
Your journey to better ends.
Now is your time, your season's here,
To shine brightly, and without fear.

Stay blessed, embrace the Light.
Without their darkness, your future is incredibly
bright.

Ephemeral Embrace

In shadows dark where ravens soar,
With whispered words and nothing more,
You touched my heart with careless ease,
A passing fancy, brief to please.

I dreamt of endless love divine,
While you sought pleasure for a time,
My soul aflame with passion true,
Yours cold as moonlight's pallid hue.

Our paths entwined like dying leaves,
My heart now broken, yours receives
No tremor of remorse or pain,
For what was lost, what might remain.

I built our castle in the air,
While you knew not, nor did you care,
That someday soon the winds would blow,
And all my dreams would surely go.

My love was like the steadfast sea,
Yours shallow as the tide could be,
I offered stars that shine above,
You gave but shadows, never love.

Now ghostlike through my life you fade,
A remnant of the choice I made,
You'll never see what you let slip,
Like blood from Death's own crimson lip.

The pendulum of fate swings wide,
As loneliness creeps at your side,
For you know what you have done,
In losing me, you've nothing won.

Your absence haunts like midnight bell,
My empty heart, a living hell,
The raven croaks forevermore,
Your name upon my chamber door.

The Quest

Paradoxical the victim,
To cycle in, out, then back again.
For me, true connection is a rare,
Precious gem.

Never again will I settle ,
Not for something less,
In matters of the heart,
I will not acquiesce.

I'd rather wait in isolation,
A lifetime long.
Avoid repeating the same mistakes,
Rushing into something wrong.

To feel truly captivated,
That's my quest,
Not just to feel needed,
but to find the best.

Each fleeting moment,
Not worth the hold.
Wasted on something so ordinary,
Someone so unspeakably cold.

I yearn for the extraordinary,
That heartfelt desire
A love that illuminates,
Two souls set afire

So here I stand, patient,
Eyes afire.
Refusing the mundane,
Yearning higher.

That true connection,
When it finally comes through.
Will be worth every lonely moment,
That I gladly knew.

A Ballad of Shattered Trust

Your smile, a weapon, sharp and bright,
Engagement's dance, the sweetest plight.
A trust misplaced, a heart laid bare,
Now wounded deep, beyond repair.

You played the game, a master's hand,
Each move you made, a well-laid plan.
At first I thought, you were my sun,
Warming my soul, the chosen one.

But shadows hid, behind your eyes,
Your kisses cloaked, in crafty lies.
And though I gave, my love so free,
You turned my love, to mockery.

My heart, now cold, a fortress walled,
Foreboding gates, forever called.
No trespass now, no tender touch,
For fear it all becomes too much.

This was your aim, your cruel design,
To win the game, my trust malign.
And now you sleep, with ease so sweet,
While tears my pillow nightly greet.

So, here's your prize, your gleaming crown,
A victory draped in my renown.
Congrats, you won, a hollow gain,
In breaking me, in causing pain.

The Dance of Betrayal

In shadows where two hearts may stray,
Their dance in secrecy does weave,
A tale where one may drift away,
And promises are left to grieve.

A partner true knows how to hold,
The essence of a cherished bond,
With boundaries set and grace untold,
Their loyalty grows deeply fond.

Yet when another tempts the night,
Their presence whispers of deceit,
It's not the stranger birthed in spite,
But one who wavers at their feet.

For if a heart can turn that way,
It bears the seed of treachery,
While knowing hands that lead astray,
Share in the ache of infamy.

Respect the ties of love unbent,
And honor borders set to shield,
For those who act with kind intent,
True prizes time will yield.

Do not compete with a roving soul,
That sees your worth as some play,
A partner steadfast, who is whole,
Will shun the lure and choose to stay.

You cannot mend a heart that breaks,
Nor anchor one that will not stay,
For love that's true and boundless makes,
Its own resolve to never sway.

Reminder

In the silence of the night, we find our strength,
A reminder echoes, stretching far in length.
We are not the keepers of others' cruel ways,
Their gaslighting, their games, their evil plays.

Their manipulation, unkindness, and deceit,
These are burdens they alone must meet.
For in our hearts, a truth we hold dear,
We are not to blame for their actions, their fear.

What lies within our grasp, our gentle hands,
Is how we respond, where we make our stands.
To set boundaries firm, to know our worth,
To protect the peace that gives our soul its birth.

We choose to rise above, to not be swayed,
By shadows cast from games they've played.
Let their actions fall away, like leaves in the
breeze,
We'll stand tall, with grace, with ease.

For we are beautiful, resilient, and strong,
In our hearts, we know we belong.

Why Johnny Cash?

Beware those whose smile draws all near,
With allure, the mask, the hidden sneer.
They'll make you feel at ease, so warm.
Yet behind them leave a trail, a perfect storm.

Their actions sow chaos, hearts distraught, Playing
with emotions, caring not.
No one sees the depths of their deceit,
Except those they choose to mistreat.

A false sense of closeness this bestows,
Like a vampire, not of blood, but souls.
Their smile, their eyes, a crafted guise,
A facade that hides the truth inside.

Take and take, yet it's never enough,
Blaming others for their own rough.
Draining them till they're but a shell,
Then casting them aside, a living hell.

They tell the world it was your fault,
Your efforts, your love, all for naught.
Walking through life without a care,
No regret, no remorse, no despair.

I pity you, for your hollow pride,
One day, you'll have nowhere to hide.
For every action, there's a cost,
And one day, your soul will be lost.

In the deafening silence, a Star falls down
You can run on for a long time,
The Seven Trumpets sound,
Sooner or later God will cut you down.

Yearning Embrace

If ever you need to lay down on my chest,
And cover it in tears, I will gladly let you rest.
I'll hold you close, until you fall asleep,
In my arms, your secrets safe to keep.

I long for someone to share my days and nights,
To be the one who soothes your deepest plights.
I wish your happiest moments to be with me,
And be your home for dark things, too, you see.

In joy and sorrow, in laughter and in pain,
With you, my love, I will always remain.
For I yearn to be the one you turn to,
In every moment, to be there for you.

Disrespect

You never change, now listen here,
Your place isn't with me, go, disappear.
No common decency, no respect,
Has severed the ties you seem to expect.

Blame me for basic boundary lines,
It won't absolve your hateful signs.
Disrespect, bullying, is what you do,
Go ahead, blame me if that comforts you.

Cruelty fed by arrogance bold,
Your hollow heart, it leaves me cold.
Immature, coward's easy route,
But what's inside will filter out.

Entitlement and no remorse,
You chose this dark and winding course.
I'm not at fault for who you are,
It's clear you've chased the brightest star.

Your blame misplaced, your thoughts askew,
Time to face the truth that's due.
Seek therapy, heal your mental strain,
Respect is earned, not won in vain.

Love's Elusive Embrace

Oh to be Loved in Light of Day
My heart shivers in the Night
Is there one who feels this ache?
Or am I alone in this plight?

I chase shadows, hearts afar
Hoping one will feel the same
Yet each step brings only scars
And my soul grows more in shame

In Love's Garden, I sow seeds
Watering with my earnest tears
None will sprout, my spirit pleads
Unseen through the silent years

In my hands, a cactus blooms
Thorns that pierce but show no care
Just to feel Love, through these dooms
I'd embrace it, unaware

Do I ask for too much Grace
Or not Enough, I cannot say
Love's elusive, fleeting face
Haunts me night and haunts me day

Kindness, goodness, all in vain
Still my worth seems but a ghost
In this aching, endless pain,
I feel lost, more than most.

I hate that I still miss you

I hate that I still miss you, every single night,
I close my eyes but can't escape the fight.
My body aches, my heart is torn,
For someone who's left me so forlorn.

You don't talk, you don't think of me at all,
Yet here I am, losing sleep, feeling small.
Discarded, forgotten, like I meant nothing,
While I'm left with these thoughts, constantly
bluffing.

Half a month has passed, but pain remains,
I'm drowning in memories, wrapped in chains.
You made me feel loved, then threw me aside,
Now I'm lost, with no place to hide.

It's 6 p.m., I just got out of bed,
Wishing these thoughts would leave my head.
I hate that I'm still here, feeling this way,
Longing for someone who won't even stay.

You Win

In shadows deep, your whispers sang,
The game you played, a venomous tang.
You won, you broke me, piece by piece,
My heart now cold from your caprice.

An actor skilled on love's stage,
You weaved, you spun, entrapped my cage.
You deserve an award so grand,
For fooling this once-trusting hand.

I thought you were the chosen one,
A love, a light, a rising sun.
But in your eyes, I saw the night,
My trust now shattered, out of sight.

The plan was set, to see me fall,
My dreams now dust, my heart a thrall.
While you sleep sound in victories' keep,
Upon my pillow, teardrops seep.

Congrats to you, the game is done,
In this dark tale, you're the one.
But in the end, who truly lost?
The prize of pain, the winning cost.

Until it's gone

Some people don't know what they have until it's
gone,
But what about the ones who do?
The ones who never took a damn thing for
granted,
Who cherished every moment, every breath, every
view.

They held on with all their might,
Fought against the tide,
Yet watched helplessly as it slipped away,
The love they couldn't hide.

Isn't it so much worse for them?
To know the value, to feel the pain,
To see the light fade into darkness,
And stand alone in the rain.

For those who knew, who truly cared,
The loss cuts deeper, the wound laid bare.
They loved with all their heart and soul,
Only to bear a scar where love left a hole.

Made in the USA
Monee, IL
07 July 2026

56551330R00075